I0762631

Over-the-Top Animals
Biggest Ape
By Suzane Nguyen
BLASTOFF! BEGINNERS, AN IMPRINT OF BELLWETHER MEDIA BY FLUTTERBEE
BLASTOFF! Beginners

Blastoff! Beginners are developed by literacy experts and educators to meet the needs of early readers. These engaging informational texts support young children as they begin reading about their world. Through simple language and high frequency words paired with crisp, colorful photos, Blastoff! Beginners launch young readers into the universe of independent reading.

Sight Words in This Book

a	can	help	one	they
are	eat	it	people	too
as	get	long	the	
be	go	must	their	
big	have	on	them	

This edition first published in 2027 by Bellwether Media, Inc.

For information regarding permission, write to Bellwether Media, Inc., Attention: Permissions Department, 3500 American Blvd W, Suite 150, Bloomington, MN 55431.

Library of Congress Cataloging-in-Publication Data is available at www.loc.gov or upon request from the publisher.

ISBN: 9798898800048 (hardcover)
ISBN: 9798898801403 (ebook)

Editor: Betsy Rathburn Designer: Laura Sowers

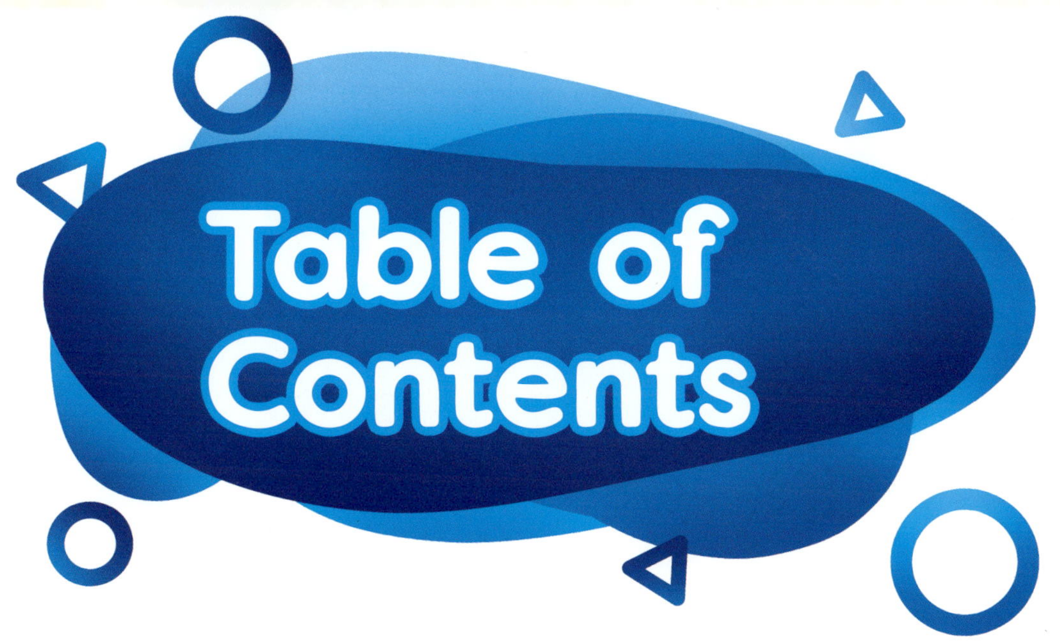
Table of Contents

Walking Tall

A gorilla
walks tall.
It hits its **chest**!

chest

Tall and Strong

Gorillas are big. They are the biggest **apes**!

They are strong.
They break branches.
They get fruit.

Gorillas stand tall. They can grow as tall as people.

They have
long arms.
They have
big stomachs too.

Big Eaters

Gorillas must be big. They keep one another safe.

Their long arms
are strong.
They walk on them.

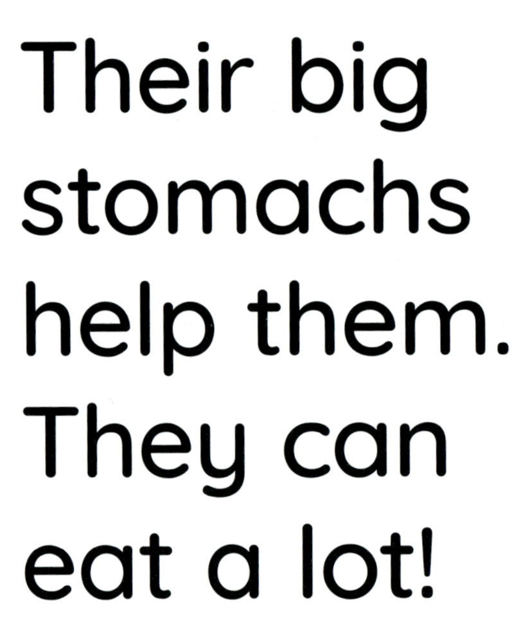

Their big stomachs help them. They can eat a lot!

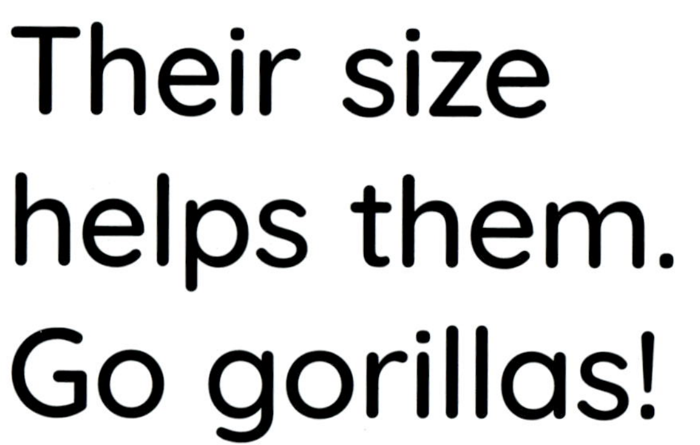

Their size
helps them.
Go gorillas!

The Biggest Ape

Body Parts

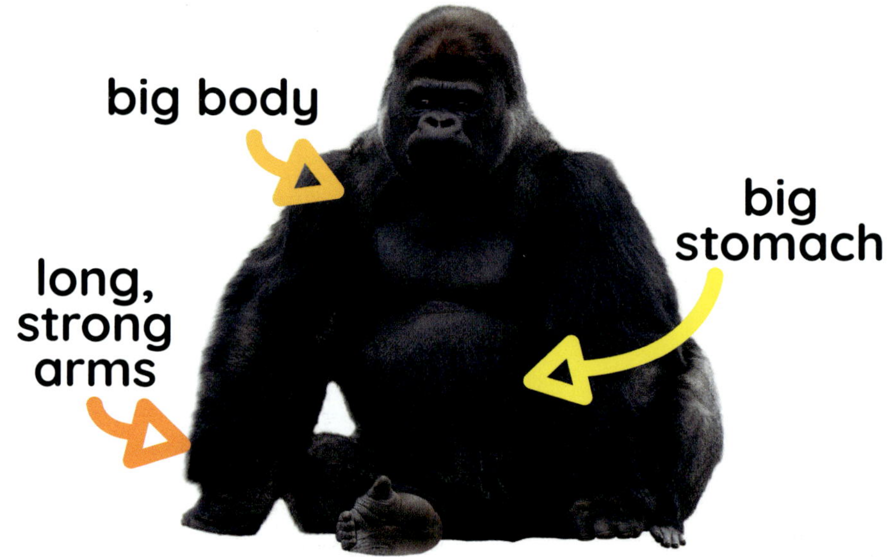

Using Their Size

keep one another safe

walk on arms

eat a lot

Glossary

apes

large animals similar to monkeys but without tails

chest

the part of a gorilla's body that is between its neck and stomach

To Learn More

ON THE WEB

FACTSURFER

Factsurfer.com gives you a safe, fun way to find more information.

1. Go to www.factsurfer.com.

2. Enter "biggest ape" into the search box and click 🔍.

3. Select your book cover to see a list of related content.

Index

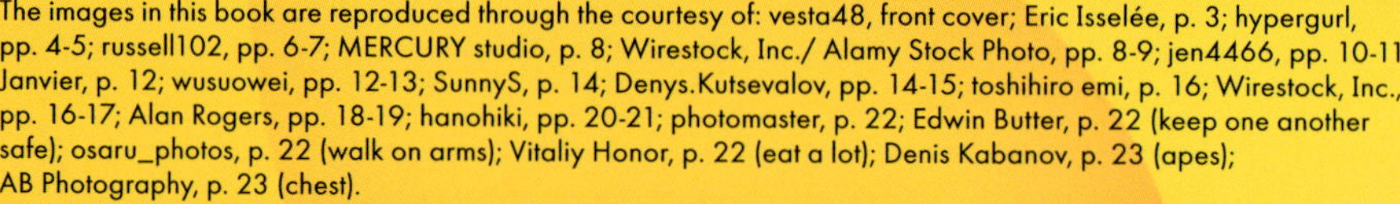

The images in this book are reproduced through the courtesy of: vesta48, front cover; Eric Isselée, p. 3; hypergurl, pp. 4-5; russell102, pp. 6-7; MERCURY studio, p. 8; Wirestock, Inc./ Alamy Stock Photo, pp. 8-9; jen4466, pp. 10-11; Janvier, p. 12; wusuowei, pp. 12-13; SunnyS, p. 14; Denys.Kutsevalov, pp. 14-15; toshihiro emi, p. 16; Wirestock, Inc., pp. 16-17; Alan Rogers, pp. 18-19; hanohiki, pp. 20-21; photomaster, p. 22; Edwin Butter, p. 22 (keep one another safe); osaru_photos, p. 22 (walk on arms); Vitaliy Honor, p. 22 (eat a lot); Denis Kabanov, p. 23 (apes); AB Photography, p. 23 (chest).